GW00578230

SCOTTISH POEMS AND BALLADS

JARROLD POETS SERIES

Also in this series:

William Wordsworth
Samuel Taylor Coleridge
Percy Bysshe Shelley
John Keats
Robert and Elizabeth Browning
Alfred Lord Tennyson
Rudyard Kipling
The War Poets
The Lady Poets
Robert Burns

ANTHOLOGY OF SCOTTISH POEMS AND BALLADS

Poems selected by Mrs E McBeath.
Designed and produced by Parke Sutton Publishing Limited, Norwich
for Jarrold Publishing, Norwich.
First published 1992

ISBN 0-7117-0403-1

CONTENTS

PROUD MAISIE

(From *The Heart of Midlothian*)

Proud Maisie is in the wood,
  Walking so early;
Sweet Robin sits on the bush,
  Singing so rarely.

"Tell me, thou bonny bird,
  When shall I marry me?"
"When six braw gentlemen
  Kirkward shall carry ye."

"Who makes the bridal bed,
  Birdie, say truly?"
"The gray-headed sexton
  That delves the grave duly.

"The glow-worm o'er grave and stone
  Shall light thee steady.
The owl from the steeple sing,
  'Welcome, proud lady.'"

BORDER MARCH

March, march, Ettrick, and Teviotdale,
    Why the deil dinna ye march forward in order?
March, march, Eskdale and Liddesdale,
     All the Blue Bonnets are bound for the Border.
       Many a banner spread,
       Flutters above your head,
     Many a crest that is famous in story.
       Mount and make ready then,
       Sons of the mountain glen,
   Fight for the Queen and our old Scottish glory.

Come from the hills where your hirsels are grazing,
    Come from the glen of the buck and the roe;
Come to the crag where the beacon is blazing,
    Come with the buckler, the lance, and the bow.
       Trumpets are sounding,
       War-steeds are bounding,
   Stand to your arms, and march in good order;
       England shall many a day
       Tell of the bloody fray,
  When the Blue Bonnets came over the Border.

HUNTING SONG

1808

Waken, lords and ladies gay,
On the mountain dawns the day,
All the jolly chase is here,
With hawk, and horse, and hunting-spear!
Hounds are in their couples yelling,
Hawks are whistling, horns are knelling,
Merrily, merrily mingle they,
"Waken, lords and ladies gay."

Waken, lords and ladies gay,
The mist has left the mountain gray,
Springlets in the dawn are steaming,
Diamonds on the brake are gleaming;
And foresters have busy been,
To track the buck in thicket green;
Now we come to chant our lay,
"Waken, lords and ladies gay."

Waken, lords and ladies gay,
To the green-wood haste away;
We can show you where he lies,
Fleet of foot, and tall of size;
We can show the marks he made,
When 'gainst the oak his antlers fray'd;
You shall see him brought to bay,
"Waken, lords and ladies gay."

Louder, louder chant the lay,
Waken, lords and ladies gay!
Tell them youth, and mirth, and glee,
Run a course as well as we;
Time, stern huntsman! who can baulk,
Stanch as hound, and fleet as hawk;
Think of this, and rise with day,
Gentle lords and ladies gay.

JOCK OF HAZELDEAN

1816

"Why weep ye by the tide, ladie?
  Why weep ye by the tide?
I'll wed ye to my youngest son,
  And ye sall be his bride:
And ye sall be his bride, ladie,
  Sae comely to be seen" –
But aye she loot the tears down fa'
  For Jock of Hazeldean.

"Now let this wilfu' grief be done,
  And dry that cheek so pale;
Young Frank is chief of Errington,
And lord of Langley-dale;
His step is first in peaceful ha',
  His sword in battle keen" –
But aye she loot the tears down fa'
  For Jock of Hazeldean.

"A chain of gold ye sall not lack,
    Nor braid to bind your hair;
Nor mettled hound, nor managed hawk,
    Nor palfrey fresh and fair;
And you, the foremost o' them a',
    Shall ride our forest queen" –
But aye she loot the tears down fa'
    For Jock of Hazeldean.

The kirk was deck'd at morning-tide,
    The tapers glimmer'd fair;
The priest and bridgroom wait the bride,
    And dame and knight are there.
They sought her baith by bower and ha';
    The ladie was not seen!
She's o'er the Border and awa,
    Wi' Jock of Hazeldean.

LOCHINVAR

Lady Heron's Song

O, young Lochinvar is come out of the west,
Through all the wide Border his steed was the best;
And save his good broadsword he weapons had none,
He rode all unarm'd, and he rode all alone.
So faithful in love, and so dauntless in war,
There never was knight like the young Lochinvar.

He staid not for brake, and he stopp'd not for stone,
He swam the Eske river where ford there was none;
But ere he alighted at Netherby gate,
The bride had consented, the gallant came late:
For a laggard in love, and a dastard in war,
Was to wed the fair Ellen of brave Lochinvar.

So boldy he enter'd the Netherby Hall,
Among bride's-men, and kinsmen, and brothers, and all:
Then spoke the bride's father, his hand on his sword,
(For the poor craven bridegroom said never a word,)
"O come ye in peace here, or come ye in war,
Or to dance at our bridal, young Lord Lochinvar?" –

"I long woo'd your daughter, my suit you denied; –
Love swells like the Solway, but ebbs like its tide –
And now am I come, with this lost love of mine,
To lead but one measure, drink one cup of wine.
There are maidens in Scotland more lovely by far,
That would gladly be bride to the young Lochinvar."

The bride kiss'd the goblet: the knight took it up,
He quaff'd off the wine, and he threw down the cup.
She look'd down to blush, and she look'd up to sigh,
With a smile on her lips, and a tear in her eye.
He took her soft hand, ere her mother could bar, –
"Now tread we a measure!" said young Lochinvar.

So stately his form, and so lovely her face,
That never a hall such a galliard did grace;
While her mother did fret, and her father did fume,
And the bridegroom stood dangling his bonnet and
plume;
And the bride-maidens whisper'd, "Twere better by far,
To have match'd our fair cousin with young Lochinvar."

One touch to her hand, and one word in her ear,
When they reach'd the hall-door, and the charger stood
near;
So light to the croupe the fair lady he swung,
So light to the saddle before her he sprung!
"She is won! we are gone, over bank, bush, and scaur;
They'll have fleet steeds that follow," quoth young
* Lochinvar.*

There was mounting 'mong Græmes of the Netherby
* clan;*
Forsters, Fenwicks, and Musgraves, they rode and they
* ran:*
There was racing and chasing, on Cannobie Lee,
But the lost bride of Netherby ne'er did they see.
So daring in love, and so dauntless in war,
Have ye e'er heard of gallant like young Lochinvar?

THOMAS THE RHYMER

True Thomas lay on Huntlie bank;
   A ferlie he spied wi' his ee;
And there he saw a ladye bright,
   Come riding down by the Eildon Tree.

Her shirt was o' the grass-green silk,
Her mantle o' the velvet fyne;
At ilka tett of her horse's mane,
   Hung fifty siller bells and nine.

True Thomas he pull'd aff his cap,
   And louted low down to his knee,
"All hail, thou mighty Queen of Heaven!
   For thy peer on earth I never did see." –

"O no, O no, Thomas," she said,
   "That name does not belang to me;
I am but the Queen of fair Elfland,
   That am hither come to visit thee.

"Harp and carp, Thomas," she said;
    "Harp and carp along wi' me;
And if ye dare to kiss my lips,
    Sure of your bodie I will be." –

"Betide me weal, betide me woe,
    That weird shall never daunton me." –
Syne he has kiss'd her rosy lips,
    All underneath the Eildon Tree.

"Now, ye maun go wi' me," she said
    "True Thomas, ye maun go wi' me;
And ye maun serve me seven years,
    Thro' weal or woe as may chance to be."

She mounted on her milk-white steed;
    She's ta'en true Thomas up behind:
And aye, when'er her bridle rung,
    The steed flew swifter than the wind.

O they rade on, and farther on;
    The steed gaed swifter than the wind;
Until they reach'd a desert wide,
    And living land was left behind.

"Light down, light down, now, true Thomas,
    And lean your head upon my knee;
Abide and rest a little space,
    And I will shew you ferlies three.

"O see ye not yon narrow road,
    So thick beset with thorns and briers?
That is the path of righteousness,
    Though after it but few enquires.

"And see ye not that braid braid road,
    That lies across that lily leven?
That is the path of wickedness,
    Though some call it the road to heaven.

"And see not ye that bonny road,
    That winds about the fernie brae?
That is the road to fair Elfland,
    Where thou and I this night maun gae.

"But, Thomas, ye maun hold your tongue,
    Whatever ye may hear or see;
For, if ye speak word in Ellflyn land.
    Ye'll ne'er get back to your ain countrie."

O they rade on, and farther on,
    And they waded through rivers aboon the knee,
And they saw neither sun nor moon,
    But they heard the roaring of the sea.

It was mirk mirk night, and there was nae stern light,
    And they waded through red blude to the knee;
For a' the blude that's shed on earth
    Rins through the springs o' that countrie.

Syne they came on to a garden green,
    And she pu'd an apple frae a tree —
"Take this for thy wages, true Thomas;
    It will give thee the tongue that can never lie." —

"My tongue is mine ain," true Thomas said;
   "A gudely gift ye wad gie to me!
I neither dought to buy nor sell,
   At fair or tryst where I may be.

"I dought neither speak to prince or peer,
   Nor ask of grace from fair ladye." –
"Now hold thy peace!" the lady said,
   "For as I say, so must it be." –

He has gotten a coat of the even cloth,
   And a pair of shoes of velvet green;
And till seven years were gane and past,
   True Thomas on earth was never seen.

ELSPETH'S BALLAD

Now haud your tongue, baith wife and carle,
  And listen, great and sma',
And I will sing of Glenallan's Earl
  That fought on the red Harlaw.

The cronach's cried on Bennachie,
  And doun the Don and a',
And hieland and lawland may mournfu' be
  For the sair field of Harlaw.

They saddled a hundred milk-white steeds,
  They hae bridled a hundred black,
With a chafron of steel on each horse's head,
  And a good knight upon his back.

They hadna ridden a mile, a mile,
  A mile, but barely ten,
When Donald came branking down the brae
  Wi' twenty thousand men.

Their tartans they were waving wide,
  Their glaives were glancing clear,
The pibrochs rung frae side to side,
  Would deafen ye to hear.

The great Earl in his stirrups stood,
  That Highland host to see;
Now here a knight that's stout and good
  May prove a jeopardie:

"What would'st thou do, my squire so gay,
  That rides beside my reyne,
Were ye Glennallan's Earl the day,
  And I were Roland Cheyne?

"To turn the rein were sin and shame,
  To fight were wond'rous peril;
What would ye do now, Roland Cheyne,
  Were ye Glenallan's Earl?'

"Were I Glenallan's Earl this tide,
    And ye were Roland Cheyne,
The spur should be in my horse's side,
    And the bridle upon his mane.

"If they hae twenty thousand blades,
    And we twice ten times ten,
Yet they hae but their tartan plaids,
    and we are mail-clad men.

"My horse shall ride through ranks sae rude,
    As through the moorland fern, –
Then ne'er let the gentle Norman blude
    Grow cauld for Highland kerne."

Oh, Say Not, My Love

Oh, say not, my love, with that mortified air,
  That your spring-time of pleasure is flown,
Nor bid me to maids that are younger repair,
  For those raptures that still are thine own.

Though April his temples may wreathe with the vine,
  Its tendrils in infancy curl'd,
'Tis the ardour of August matures us the wine,
  Whose life-blood enlivens the world.

Though thy form, that was fashion'd as light as a fay's,
  Has assumed a proportion more round,
And thy glance, that was bright as a falcon's at gaze
  Looks soberly now on the ground, –

Enough, after absence to meet me again,
  Thy steps still with ecstasy move;
Enough, that those dear sober glances retain
  For me the kind language of love.

FROM THE BETROTHED

SOLDIER WAKE

Soldier, wake! the day is peeping;
Honour ne'er was won in sleeping,
Never when the sunbeams still
Lay unreflected on the hill:
'Tis when they are glinted back
From axe and armour, spear and jack,
That they promise future story,
Many a page of deathless glory.
Shileds that are the foeman's terror,
Ever are the morning's mirror.

Arm and up! the morning beam
Hath call'd the rustic to his team,
Hath call'd the falc'ner to the lake,
Hath call'd the hunstman to the brake;
The early student ponders o'er
His dusty tomes of ancient lore.
Soldier, wake! thy harvest, fame;
Thy study, conquest; war, thy game.
Shield, that would be foeman's terror,
Still should gleam the morning's mirror.

Poor hire repays the rustic's pain;
More paltry still the sportsman's gain;
Vainest of all, the student's theme
Ends in some metaphysic dream:
Yet each is up, and each has toil'd
Since first the peep of dawn has smiled;
And each is eagerer in his aim
Than he who barters life for fame.
Up, up, and arm thee, son of terror!
Be thy bright shield the morning's mirror.

LINES ON FORTUNE

1831

Fortune, my Foe, why dost thou frown on me?
And will my Fortune never better be?
Wilt thou, I say, for ever breed my pain?
And wilt thou ne'er return my joys again?

No – let my ditty be henceforth –

Fortune, my Friend, how well thou favourest me!
A kinder Fortune man did never see!
Thou propp'st my thigh, thou ridd'st my knee of pain,
I'll walk, I'll mount – I'll be a man again. –

FROM THE LORD OF THE ISLES

Oh, War! thou hast thy fierce delight,
Thy gleams of joy, intensely bright!
Such gleams, as from thy polish'd shield
Fly dazzling o'er the battle-field!
Such transports wake, severe and high,
Amid the pealing conquestcry;
Scarce less, when, after battle lost,
Muster the remnants of a host,
And as each comrade's name they tell,
Who in the well-fought conflict fell,
Knitting stern brow o'er flashing eye,
Vow to avenge them or to die! –
Warriors! – and where are warriors found,
If not on martial Britain's ground?
And who, when waked with note of fire,
Love more than they the British lyre? –

Know ye not, — hearts to honour dear!
That joy, deep-thrilling, stern, severe,
At which the heartstrings vibrate high,
And wake the fountains of the eye?
And blame ye, then, the Bruce, if trace
Or tear is on his manly face,
When, scanty relics of the train
That hail'd at Scone his early reign,
This patriot band around him hung,
And to his knees and bosom clung? —
Blame ye the Bruce? — his brother blamed,
But shared the weakness, while ashamed,
With haughty laugh his head he turn'd,
And dash'd away the tear he scorn'd.

On the Massacre of Glencoe

"O tell me, Harper, wherefore flow
Thy wayward notes of wail and woe,
Far down the desert of Glencoe,
    Where none may list their melody?
Say, harp'st thou to the mists that fly,
Or to the dun-deer glancing by,
Or to the eagle, that from high
    Screams chorus to thy minstrelsy?"

"No, not to these, for they have rest, –
The mist-wreath has the mountain-crest,
The stag his lair, the erne her nest,
    Abode of lone security.
But those for whom I pour the lay,
Not wild-wood deep, nor mountain gray,
Not this deep dell, that shrouds from day,
    Could screen from treach'rous cruelty.

"Their flag was furl'd, and mute their drum,
The very household dogs were dumb,
Unwont to bay at guests that come
    In guise of hospitalty.
His blithest notes the piper plied,
Her gayest snood the maiden tied,
The dame her distaff flung aside,
   To tend her kindly housewifery.

"The hand that mingled in the meal,
At midnight drew the felon steel,
And gave the host's kind breast to feel
   Meed for his hospitality!
The friendly hearth which warm'd that hand,
At midnight arm'd it with the brand,
That bade destruction's flames expand
   Their red and fearful blazonry.

"Then woman's shriek was heard in vain,
Nor infancy's unpitied plain,
More than the warrior's groan, could gain
    Respite from ruthless butchery!
The winter wind that whistled shrill,
The snows that night that cloked the hill,
Though wild and pitiless, had still
    Far more than Southern clemency.

"Long have my harp's best notes been gone,
Few are its strings, and faint their tone,
They can but sound in desert lone
    Their gray-hair'd master's misery.
Were each gray hair a minstrel string,
Each chord should imprecations fling,
Till startled Scotland loud should ring,
    'Revenge for blood and treachery!'"

MacGregor's Gathering

1816

The moon's on the lake, and the mist's on the brae,
And the Clan has a name that is nameless by day;
   Then gather, gather, gather,
    Grigalach!
  Gather, gather, gather etc.

Our signal for fight, that from monarchs we drew,
Must be heard but by night in our vengeful haloo!
   Then haloo, Grigalach! haloo,
    Grigalach!
  Haloo, haloo, haloo, Grigalach, etc.

Glen Orchy's proud mountains, Coalchuirn and her
  towers,
Glenstrae and Glenlyon no longer are ours;
  We're landless, landless, landless, Grigalach!
  Landless, landless, landless, etc.

But doom'd and devoted by vassal and lord,
MacGregor has still both his heart and his sword!
    Then courage, courage, courage, Grigalach!
    Courage, courage, courage, etc.

If they rob us of name and pursue us with beagles,
Give their roofs to the flame, and their flesh to the eagles!
    Then vengeance, vengeance, vengeance, Grigalach!
    Vengeance, vengeance, vengeance, etc.

While there's leaves in the forest, and foam on the river,
MacGregor, despite them, shall flourish for ever!
    Come then Grigalach, come then, Grigalach,
    Come then, come then, come then etc.

Through the depths of Loch Katrine the steed shall career,
O'er the peak of Ben-Lomond the galley shall steer,
And the rocks of Craig-Royston like icicles melt,
Ere our wrongs be forgot, or our vengeance unfelt!
    Then gather, gather, gather, Grigalach!
    Gather, gather, gather, etc.

SONG

Air – The Bonnets of Bonny Dundee.

To the Lords of Convention 'twas Claver'se who spoke,
"Ere the King's crown shall fall there are crowns to be broke;
So let each Cavalier who loves honour and me,
Come follow the bonnet of Bonny Dundee.

"Come fill up my cup, come fill up my can,
Come saddle your horses, and call up your men;
Come open the West Port, and let me gang free,
And it's room for the bonnets of Bonny Dundee!"

Dundee he is mounted, he rides up the street,
The bells are rung backward, the drums they are beat;
But the Provost, douce man, said, "Just e'en let him be,
The Gude Town is weel quit of that Deil of Dundee."
    Come fill up my cup, etc.

As he rode down the sanctified bends of the Bow,
Ilk carline was flyting and shaking her pow;
But the young plants of grace they look'd couthie and slee,
Thinking, luck to thy bonnet, thou Bonny Dundee!
    Come fill up my cup, etc.

With sour-featured Whigs the Grassmarket was cramm'd
As if half the West had set tryst to be hang'd;
There was spite in each look, there wass fear in each e'e,
As they watch'd for the bonnets of Bonny Dundee.
    Come fill up my cup, etc.

These cowls of Kilmarnock had spits and had spears,
And lang-hafted gullies to kill Cavaliers;
But they shrunk to close-heads, and the causeway was free,
At the toss of the bonnet of Bonny Dundee.
    Come fill up my cup, etc.

He spurr'd to the foot of the proud Castle rock,
And with the gay Gordon he gallantly spoke;
"Let Mons Meg and her marrows speak twa words or three,
For the love of the bonnet of Bonny Dundee."
    Come fill up my cup, etc.

The Gordon demands of him which way he goes –
"Where'er shall direct me the shade of Montrose!
Your Grace in short space shall hear tidings of me,
Or that low lies the bonnet of Bonny Dundee."
    Come fill up my cup, etc.

"There are hills beyond Pentland, and lands beyond Forth,
If there's lords in the Lowlands, there's chiefs in the North;
There are wild Duniewassals three thousand times three,
Will cry hoigh! for the bonnet of Bonny Dundee."
    Come fill up my cup, etc.

"There's brass on the target of barken'd bull-hide;
There's steel in the scabbard that dangles beside;
The brass shall be burnish'd, the steel shall flash free,
At a toss of the bonnet of Bonny Dundee."
    Come fill up my cup, etc.

"Away to the hills, to the caves, to the rocks —
Ere I own an usurper, I'll couch with the fox;
And tremble, false Whigs, in the midst of your glee,
You have not seen the last of my bonnet and me!"
    Come fill up my cup, etc.

He waved his proud hand, and the trumpets were blown,
The kettle-drums clash'd, and the horsemen rode on,
Till on Ravelston's cliffs and on Clermiston's lee,
Died away the wild war-notes of Bonny Dundee.

Come fill up my cup, come fill up my can,
Come saddle the horses and call up the men,
Come open your gates, and let me gae free,
For it's up with the bonnets of Bonny Dundee!

FOR A' THAT AN' A' THAT

Though right be aft put down by strength,
  As mony a day we saw that,
The true and leilfu' cause at length
  Shall bear the grie for a' that.
For a' that an' a' that,
  Guns, guillotines, and a' that,
The Fleur-de-lis, that lost her right,
  Is queen again for a' that!

We'll twine her in a friendly knot
  With England's Rose, and a' that;
The Shamrock shall not be forgot,
  For Wellington made braw that.
The Thistle, though her leaf be rude,
  Yet faith we'll no misca' that,
She shelter'd in her solitude
  The Fleur-de-lis, for a' that.

The Austrian Vine, the Prussian Pine
    (For Blucher's sake, hurra that,)
The Spanish Olive, too, shall join,
    And bloom in peace for a' that.
Stout Russia's Hemp, so surely twined
    Around our wreath we'll draw that,
And he that would the cord unbind,
    Shall have it for his gra-vat!

Or, if to choke sae puir a sot,
    Your pity scorn to thraw that,
The Devil's elbow be his lot,
    Where he may sit and claw that.
In psite of slight, in spite of might,
    In spite of brags, an' a' that,
The lads that battled for the right,
    Have won the day, an' a' that!

There's ae bit spot I had forgot,
    America they ca' that!
A coward plot her rats had got
    Their father's flag to gnaw that:
Now see it fly top-gallant high,
    Atlantic winds shall blaw that,
And Yankee loon, beware your croun,
    There's kames in hand to claw that!

For on the land, or on the sea,
    Where'er the breezes blaw that,
The British Flag shall bear the grie,
    And win the day for a' that!

INTRODUCTION TO CANTO FIRST

From *Marmion*

To William Stewart Rose, Esq.
Ashetiel, Ettrick Forest

November's sky is chill and drear,
November's leaf is red and sear:
Late, gazing down the steepy linn,
That hems our little garden in.
Low in its dark and narrow glen,
You scarce the rivulet might ken,
So thick the tangled greenwood grew,
So feeble trill'd the streamlet through:
Now, murmuring hoarse, and frequent seen
Through bush and brier, no longer green,
An angry brook, it sweeps the glade,
Brawls over rock and wild cascade,
And, foaming brown with doubled speed,
Hurries its waters to the Tweed.

No longer Autumn's glowing red
Upon our Forest hills is shed;
No more, beneath the evening beam,
Fair Tweed reflects their purple gleam;
Away hath pass'd the heather-bell
That bloom'd so rich on Needpath-fell;
Sallow his brow, and russet bare
Are now the sister-heights of Yair.
The sheep, before the pinching heaven,
To shelter'd dale and down are driven,
Where yet some faded herbage pines,
And yet a watery sunbeam shines:
In meek despondency they eye
The wither'd sward and wintry sky,
And far beneath their summer hill,
Stray sadly by Glenkinnon's rill:
The shepherd shifts his mantle's fold,
And wraps him closer from the cold;
His dogs, no merry circles wheel,
But, shivering, follow at his heel;
A cowering glance they often cast,
As deeper moans the gathering blast.

My imps, though hardy, bold, and wild,
As best befits the mountain child,
Feel the sad influence of the hour,
And wail the daisy's vanished flower;
Their summer gambols tell, and mourn,
And anxious ask, – Will spring return,
And birds and lambs again be gay,
And blossoms clothe the hawthorn spray?

Yes, prattlers, yes. The daisy's flower
Again shall paint your summer bower;
Again the hawthorn shall supply
The garlands you delight to tie;
The lambs upon the lea shall bound,
The wild birds carol to the round,
And while you frolic light as they,
Too short shall seem the summer day.

FROM THE LAY OF THE LAST MINSTREL

INTRODUCTION

The way was long, the wind was cold,
The Minstrel was infirm and old;
His wither'd cheek, and tresses gray,
Seem'd to have known a better day;
The harp, his sole remaining joy,
Was carried by an orphan boy.
The last of all the Bards was he,
Who sung of Border chivalry;
For, welladay! their date was fled,
His tuneful brethren all were dead;
And he, neglected and oppress'd,
Wish'd to be with them, and at rest.
No more on prancing palfrey borne,
He caroll'd, light as lark at morn;
No longer courted and caress'd

High placed in hall, a welcome guest,
He pour'd, to lord and lady gay,
The unpremeditated lay:
Old times were changed, old manners gone;
A stranger fill'd the Stuarts' throne;
The bigots of the iron time
Had call'd his harmless art a crime.
A wandering Harper, scorn'd and poor,
He begg'd his bread from door to door.
Amnd tuned, to please a peasant's ear,
The harp, a king had loved to hear.

　He pass'd where Newark's stately tower
Looks out from Yarrow's birchen bower:
The Minstrel gazed with wishful eye –
No humbler resting-place was nigh,
With hesitating step at last,
The embattled portal arch he pass'd,
Whose ponderous grate and massy bar
Had oft roll'd back the tide of war,
But never closed the iron door
Against the desolate and poor.

The Duchess marked his weary pace,
His timid mien, and reverend face,
And bade her page the menials tell,
That they should tend the old man well:
For she had known adversity,
Though born in such a high degree;
In pride of power, in beauty's bloom,
Had wept o'er Monmouth's bloody tomb!

When kindness had his wants supplied,
And the old man was gratified,
Began to rise his minstrel pride:
And he began to talk anon,
Of good Earl Francis, dead and gone,
And of Earl Walter, rest him, God!
A braver ne'er to battle rode;
And how full many a tale he knew,
Of the old warriors of Buccleuch:
And, would the noble Duchess deign
To listen to an old man's strain,
Though stiff his hand, his voice though weak,
He thought even yet, the sooth to speak,
That, if she loved the harp to hear,
He could make music to her ear.

The humble boon was soon obtain'd;
The Aged Minstrel audience gain'd.
But, when he reach'd the room of state,
Where she, with all her ladies, sate,
Perchance he wish'd his boon denied:
For, when to tune his harp he tried,
His trembling hand had lost the ease,
Which marks security to please;
And scenes, long past, of joy and pain,
Came wildering o'er his aged brain –
He tried to tune his harp in vain!

The pitying Duchess praised its chime,
And gave him heart, and gave him time,
Till every string's according glee
Was blended into harmony.
And then, he said, he would full fain
He could recall an ancient strain,
He never thought to sing again.
It was not framed for village churls,
But for high dames and mighty earls;
He had play'd it to King Charles the Good,
When he kept court in Holyrood;
And much he wish'd, yet fear'd, to try

The long-forgotten melody.
Amid the strings his fingers stray'd,
And an uncertain warbling made,
And oft he shook his hoary head.
But when he caught the measure wild,
The old man raised his face, and smiled;
And lighten'd up his faded eye,
With all a poet's ecstasy!
In varying cadence, soft or strong,
He swept the sounding chords along:
The present scene, the future lot,
His toils, his wants, were all forgot:
Cold diffidence, and age's frost,
In the full tide of song were lost;
Each blank, in faithless memory void,
The poet's glowing thought supplied;
And, while his harp responsive rung,
'Twas thus the LATEST MINSTREL *sung.*

Canto Sixth

I

Breathes there the man, with soul so dead,
Who never to himself hath said,
　　This is my own, my native land!
Whose heart hath ne'er within him burn'd,
As home his footsteps he hath turn'd,
　　From wandering on a foreign strand!
If such there breathe, go, mark him well;
For him no Minstrel raptures swell;
High though his titles, proud his name,
Boundless his wealth as wish can claim;
Despite those titles, power, and pelf,
The wretch, concentred all in self,
Living, shall forfeit fair renown,
And, doubly dying, shall go down
To the vile dust, from whence he sprung
Unwept, unhonour'd and unsung.

II

O Caledonia! stern and wild,
Meet nurse for a poetic child!
Land of brown heath and shaggy wood,
Land of the mountain and the flood,
Land of my sires! what mortal hand
Can e'er untie the filial band,
That knits me to thy rugged strand!
Still, as I view each well-known scene,
Think what is now, and what hath been,
Seems as, to me, of all bereft,
Sole friends thy woods and streams were left;
And thus I love them better still,
Even in extremity of ill.
By Yarrow's streams still let me stray,
Though none should guide my feeble way;
Still feel the breeze down Ettrick break,
Although it chill my wither'd cheek;
Still lay my head by Teviot Stone,
Though there, forgotten and alone,
The Bard may draw his parting groan.

ROBERT LOUIS STEVENSON

BLOCK CITY

What are you able to build with your blocks?
Castles and palaces, temples and docks.
Rain may keep raining, and others go roam,
But I can be happy and building at home.

Let the sofa be mountains, the carpet be sea,
There I'll establish a city for me:
A kirk and a mill and a palace beside,
And a harbour as well where my vessels may ride.

Great is the palace with pillar and wall,
A sort of a tower on the top of it all,
And steps coming down in an orderly way
To where my toy vessels lie safe in the bay.

This one is sailing and that one is moored:
Hark to the song of the sailors on board!
And see on the steps of my palace, the kings
Coming and going with presents and things!

Now I have done with it, down let it go!
All in a moment the town is laid low.
Block upon block lying scattered and free,
What is there left of my town by the sea!

Yet as I saw it, I see it again,
The kirk and the palace, the ships and the men,
And as long as I live, and where'er I may be,
I'll always remember my town by the sea.

BED IN SUMMER

In winter I get up at night
And dress by yellow candle-light.
In summer, quite the other way,
I have to go to bed by day.

I have to go to bed and see
The birds still hopping on the tree,
Or hear the grown-up people's feet
Still going past me in the street.

And does it not seem hard to you,
When all the sky is clear and blue,
And I should like so much to play,
To have to go to bed by day?

MY SHADOW

I have a little shadow that goes in and out with me,
And what can be the use of him is more than I can see.
He is very, very like me from the heels up to the head;
And I see him jump before me, when I jump into my bed.

The funniest thing about him is the way he likes to grow –
Not at all like proper children, which is always very slow;
For he sometimes shoots up taller like an india-rubber ball,
And he sometimes get so little that there's none of him
   at all.

He hasn't got a notion of how children ought to play,
And can only make a fool of me in every sort of way.
He stays so close beside me, he's a coward you can see;
I'd think shame to stick to nursie as that shadow sticks
   to me!

One morning, very early, before the sun was up,
I rose and found the shining dew on every buttercup;
By my lazy little shadow, like an arrant sleepy-head,
Had stayed at home behind me and was fast asleep in bed.

THE LAMPLIGHTER

My tea is nearly ready and the sun has left the sky;
It's time to take the window to see Leerie going by;
For every night at tea-time and before you take your seat,
With lantern and with ladder he comes posting up the
    street.

Now Tom would be a driver and Maria go to sea,
And my papa's a banker and as rich as he can be;
But I, when I am stronger and can choose what I'm to
    do,
O Leerie, I'll go round at night and light the lamps with
    you!

For we are very lucky, with a lamp before the door,
And Leerie stops to light it as he lights so many more;
And O! before you hurry by with ladder and with light,
O Leerie, see a little child and nod to him to-night!

From A Railway Carriage

Faster than fairies, faster than witches,
Bridges and houses, hedges and ditches;
And charging along like troops in a battle,
All through the meadows the horses and cattle:
All of the sights of the hill and the plain
Fly as thick as driving rain;
And ever again, in the wink of an eye,
Painted stations whistle by.

Here is a child who clambers and scrambles,
All by himself and gathering brambles;
Here is a tramp who stands and gazes;
And there is the green for stringing the daisies!
Here is a cart run away in the road
Lumping along with man and load;
And here is a mill, and there is a river:
Each a glimpse and gone for ever!

To Mrs Will H. Low

Even in the bluest noonday of July,
There could not run the smallest breath of wind
But all the quarter sounded like a wood;
And in the chequered silence and above
The hum of city cabs that sought the Bois,
Surburban ashes shivered into song.
A patter and a chatter and a chirp
And a long dying hiss – it was as though
Starched old brocaded dames though all the house
Had trailed a strident skirt, or the whole sky
Even in a wink had over-brimmed in rain.
Hark, in these shady parlours, how it talks
Of the near Autumn, how the smitten ash
Trembles and augurs floods! O not too long
In these inconstant latitudes delay,
O not too late from the unbeloved north
Trim your escape! For soon shall this low roof
Resound indeed with rain, soon shall your eyes
Search the foul garden, search the darkened rooms,
Nor find one jewel but the blazing log.

REQUIEM

Under the wide and starry sky,
Dig the grave and let me lie.
Glad did I live and gladly die,
  And I laid me down with a will.

This be the verse you grave for me:
Here he lies where he longed to be;
Home is the sailor, home from sea,
  And the hunter home from the hill.

BROWNING

Browning makes the verses:
  Your servant the critique.
Browning wouldn't sing at all:
  I fancy I could speak.
Although the book was clever
  (To give the Deil his due)
I wasn't pleased with Browning
  Nor he with my review.

FRAGMENT

Thou strainest through the mountain fern,
A most exiguously thin
> *Burn.*
For all thy foam, for all thy din,
Thee shall the pallid lake inurn,
With well-a-day for Mr Swin-
> *Burne!*
Take then this quarto in thy fin
And, O thou stoker huge and stern,
The whole affair, outside and in,
> *Burn!*
But save the true poetic kin,
The works of Mr Robert Burn!
And William Wordsworth upon Tin-
> *Tern!*

PIRATE DITTY

> From Treasure Island

Fifteen men on the Dead Man's Chest —
> *Yo-ho-ho, and a bottle of rum!*
Drink and the devil had done for the rest —
> *Yo-ho-ho, and a bottle of rum!*

UNTITLED WORKS

I have trod the upward and the downward slope;
I have endured and done in days before;
I have longed for all, and bid farewell to hope;
And I have lived and loved, and closed the door.

*

There are kind hearts still, for friends to fill
    And fools to take and break them;
But the nearest friends are the auldest friends
    And the grave's the place to seek them.

*

Fair Isle at Sea – the lovely name
Soft in my ear like music came.
That sea I loved, and once or twice
I touched at isles of Paradise.

As with heaped bees at hiving time
The boughs are clotted, as (ere prime)
Heaven swarms with stars, or the city street
Pullulates with faring feet;
So swarmed my senses once; that now
Repose behind my tranquil brow,
Unsealed, asleep, quiescent, clear,
Now only the vast shapes I hear
Hear – and my hearing slowly fills –
Rivers and winds among the twisted hills,
And hearken – and my face is lit –
Life facing; death pursuing it.

★

The morning drum-call on my eager ear
Thrills unforgotten yet; the morning dew.
Lies yet undried along my field of noon.

But now I pause at whiles in what I do,
And count the bell, and tremble lest I hear
(My work untrimmed) the sunset gun too soon.

In Autumn when the woods are red
And skies are grey and clear,
The sportsmen seek the wild fowl's bed
Or follow down the deer;
And Cupid hunts by haugh and head,
By riverside and mere,
I walk, not seeing where I tread
And keep my hearts with fear,
Sir, have an eye, on where you tread,
And keep your heart with fear,
For something lingers here;
A touch of April not yet dead,
In Autumn when the woods are red
And skies are grey and clear.

I saw red evening through the rain,
Lower above the steaming plain;
I heard the hour strike small and still,
From the black belfry on the hill.

Thought is driven out of doors to-night
By bitter memory of delight;
The sharp constraint of finger tips,
Or the shuddering touch of lips.

I heard the hour strike small and still,
From the black belfry on the hill.
Behind me I could still look down
On the outspread monstrous town.

The sharp constraint of finger tips
Or the shuddering touch of lips,
And all old memories of delight
Crowd upon my soul to-night.

Behind me I could still look down
On the outspread feverish town;
But before me still and grey
And lonely was the forward way.

My house, *I say*. But hark to the sunny doves
That make my roof the arena of their loves,
That gyre about the gable all day long
And fill the chimneys with their murmurous song:
Our house, *they say*; and *mine*, the cat declares
And spreads his golden fleece upon the chairs;
And *mine* the dog, and rises stiff with wrath
If any alien foot profane the path.
So too the buck that trimmed my terraces,
Our whilome gardener, called the garden his;
Who now, deposed, surveys my plain abode
And his late kingdom, only from the road.

*

It's an overcome sooth for age an' youth
  And it brooks wi' nae denial, `
That the dearest friends are the auldest friends
  And the young are just on trial.

There's a rival bauld wi' young an' auld
  And it's him that has bereft me;
For the sürest friends are the auldest friends
  And the maist o' mines hae left me.

Thomas Campbell

Hohenlinden

On Linden, when the sun was low,
All bloodless lay the untrodden snow;
And dark as winter was the flow
   Of Iser, rolling rapidly.

But Linden saw another sight,
When the drum beat at dead of night,
Commanding fires of death to light
   The darkness of her scenery.

By torch and trumpet fast array'd
Each horseman drew his battle blade
And furious every charger neigh'd
   To join the deadful revelry.

Then shook the hills with thunder riven,
Then rush'd the steed, to battle driven,
And louder than the bolts of Heaven
   Far flash'd the red artillery.

But redder yet that light shall glow
On Linden's hills of stainèd snow;
And bloodier yet the torrent flow
    Of Iser, rolling rapidly.

'Tis morn; but scarce yon level sun
Can pierce the war-clouds, rolling dun,
Where furious Frank and fiery Hun
    Shout in their sulphurous canopy.

The combat deepens. On ye brave
Who rush to glory, or the grave!
Wave, Munich, all thy banners wave,
    And charge with all thy chivalry!

Few, few shall part, where many meet!
The snow shall be their winding-sheet,
And every turf beneath their feet
    Shall be a soldier's sepulchre.

LORD ULLIN'S DAUGHTER

A Chieftain to the Highlands bound
  Cries 'Boatman, do not tarry!
And I'll give thee a silver pound
  To row us o'er the ferry!'

'Now who be ye, would cross Lochgyle
  This dark and stormy water?'
'O I'm the chief of Ulva's isle,
  And this, Lord Ullin's daughter.

'And fast before her father's men
  Three days we've fled together,
For should he find us in the glen,
  My blood would stain the heather.

'His horsemen hard behind us ride –
  Should they our steps discover,
Then who will cheer my bonny bride
  When they have slain her lover?'

Out spoke the hardy Highland wight,
    'I'll go, my chief, I'm ready:
It is not for your silver bright,
    But for your winsome lady:–

'And by my word! the bonny bird
    In danger shall not tarry;
So though the waves are raging white
    I'll row you o'er the ferry.'

By this the storm grew loud apace,
    The water-wraith was shrieking;
And in the scowl of heaven each face
    Grew dark as they were speaking.

But still as wilder blew the wind
    And as the night grew drearer,
Adown the glen rode armèd men,
    Their trampling sounded nearer.

'O haste thee, haste!' the lady cries,
    'Though tempests round us gather;
I'll meet the raging of the skies,
    But not an angry father.'

The boat has left a stormy land,
    A stormy sea before her, –
When, oh! too strong for human hand
    The tempest gather'd o'er her.

And still they row'd amidst the roar
    Of waters fast prevailing:
Lord Ullin reach'd that fatal shore, –
    His wrath was changed to wailing.

For, sore dismay'd, through storm and shade
    His child he did discover: –
One lovely hand she stretch'd for aid,
    And one was round her lover.

'Come back! come back!' he cried in grief
    'Across this stormy water:
And I'll forgive your Highland chief,
    My daughter! – O my daughter!'

'Twas vain: the loud waves lash'd the shore,
    Return or aid preventing:
The waters wild went o'er his child,
    And he was left lamenting.

ODE TO WINTER

When first the fiery-mantled sun
His heavenly race began to run;
Round the earth and ocean blue,
His children four the Seasons flew.
First, in green apparel dancing,
   The young Spring smiled with angel grace;
Rosy Summer next advancing,
   Rush'd into her sire's embrace –
Her bright-hair'd sire, who bade her keep
   For ever nearest to his smiles,
On Calpe's olive-shaded steep,
   On India's citron-cover'd isles:
More remote and buxom-brown,
   The Queen of vintage bow'd before his throne;
A rich pomegranate gemm'd her crown,
   A ripe sheaf bound her zone.

But howling Winter fled afar,
To hills that prop the polar star,
And loves on deer-borne car to ride,
With barren darkness by his side.
Round the shore where loud Lofoden
   Whirls to death the roaring whale,
Round the hall where Runic Odin
   Howls his war-song to the gale;
Save when adown the ravaged globe
   He travels on his native storm,
Deflowering Nature's grassy robe,
   And trampling on her faded form: –
Till light's returning lord assume
   The shaft that drives him to his polar field,
Of power to pierce his raven plume,
   And crystal-cover'd shield.

O, sire of storms! whose savage ear
The Lapland drum delights to hear,
When Frenzy with her blood-shot eye
Implores thy dreadful deity —
Archangel! power of desolation!
  Fast descending as thou art,
Say, hath mortal invocation
  Spells to touch thy stony heart?
Then, sullen Winter! hear my prayer.
  And gently rule the ruin'd year;
Nor chill the wanderer's bosom bare,
  Nor freeze the wretch's falling tear; —
To shuddering Want's unmantled bed,
  Thy horror-breathing agues cease to lend,
And gently on the orphan head
  Of innocence descend. —

But chiefly spare, O king of clouds!
The sailor on his airy shrouds;
When wrecks and beacons strew the steep,
And spectres walk along the deep.
Milder yet thy snowy breezes
   Pour on yonder tented shores,
Where the Rhine's broad billow freezes.
   Or the dark-brown Danube roars.
Oh winds of Winter! list ye there
   To many a deep and dying groan;
Or start, ye demons of the midnight air,
   At shrieks and thunders louder than your own.
Alas! e'en your unhallow'd breath
   May spare the victim fallen low;
But man will ask no truce to death, –
   No bounds to human woe.

FREEDOM AND LOVE

How delicious is the winning
Of a kiss at love's beginning,
When two mutual hearts are sighing
For the knot there's no untying!

Yet remember, 'midst your wooing,
Love has bliss, but Love has ruing;
Other smiles may make you fickle,
Tears for other charms may trickle.

Love he comes, and Love he tarries,
Just as fate or fancy carries;
Longest stays, when sorest chidden;
Laughs and flies, when press'd and bidden.

Bind the sea to slumber stilly,
Bind its odour to the lily,
Bind the aspen ne'er to quiver,
Then bind Love to last for ever.

Love's a fire that needs renewal
Of fresh beauty for its fuel:
Love's wing moults when caged and captured,
Only free, he soars enraptured.

Can you keep the bee from ranging
Or the ringdove's neck from changing?
No! nor fetter'd Love from dying
In the knot there's no untying.

JAMES HOGG

(The Ettrick Shepherd)

THE WITCH O' FIFE

Hurray, hurray, the jade's away,
Like a rocket of air with her bandalet!
I'm up in the air on my bonnie gray mare,
But I see her yet, I see her yet.
I'll ring the skirts o' the gowden wain
Wi' curb an' bit, wi' curb an' bit;
An' catch the Bear by the frozen mane —
An' I see her yet, I see her yet.

Away, away, o'er mountain an' main,
To sing at the morning's rosy yett;
An' water my mare at its fountain clear —
But I see her yet, I see her yet.
Away, thou bonnie witch o' Fife,
On foam of the air to heave an' flit,
An' little reck thou of a poet's life,
For he sees thee yet, he sees thee yet!

LINES TO SIR WALTER SCOTT BART

Sound, my old harp, thy boldest key
To strain of high festivity!
Can'st thou be silent in the brake,
Loitering by Altrive's mountain lake,
When he who gave the hand its sway
That now has tuned thee many a day,
Has gained thee honours trulier won,
Than e'er by sword of Albyn's son;
High guerdon of a soul refined,
The meed of an exalted mind?

Well suits such wreath thy loyal head,
My Counsellor, and friend indeed.
Though hard through life I've pressed my way
For many a chill and joyless day,
Since I have lived enrapt to hail
My sovereign's worth, my friend's avail,
And see, what more I prize than gain,
Our forest harp the bays obtain,
I'll ween I have not lived in vain.

Ah! could I dream when first we met,
When by the scanty ingle set,
Beyond the moors where curlews wheel
In Ettrick's bleakest, loneliest sheil,
Conning old songs of other times,
Most uncouth chants and crabbed rhymes –
Could I e'er dream that wayward wight,
Of roguish joke, and heart so light,
In whose oft-chainging eye I gazed,
Not without dread the head was crazed,
Should e'er, by genius' force alone,
Skim o'er an ocean sailed by none;
All the hid shoals of envy miss,
And gain such noble port as this?

I could not: but I cherish still
Mirth at the scene, and ever will,
When o'er the fells we took our way;
('Tis twenty years, even to a day,
Since we two sought the fabled urn
Of marble blue by Rankleburn):
No tomb appear; but oft we traced
Towns, camps, and battle-lines effaced,
Which never were, nor could remain,
Save in the bold enthusiast's brain:
The same to us — it turned our lays
To chiefs and tales of ancient days.

Deep in the rubbish under ground,
In middle of the ancient fane —
"A gallant helmet split in twain!"
The truth was obvious; but in faith
On you all words were waste of breath;
You only looked demure and sly,
And sore the brow fell o'er the eye;
You could not bear that you should ride
O'er pathless waste and forest wide,
Only to say that you had been
To see that nought was to be seen.

The evenings came; more social mirth
Ne'er flowed around the cottage hearth:
When Maitland's song first met your ear,
How the furled visage up did clear,
Beaming delight! though now a shade
Of doubt would darken into dread
That some unskilled presumptuous arm
Had marred tradition's mighty charm.

Scarce grew thy lurking dread the less,
Till she, the ancient minstrelless,
With fervid voice, and kindling eye,
And withered arms waving on high,
Sung forth these words in eldritch shriek,
While tears stood on thy nut-brown cheek –
"Na, we are nane o' the lads o' France,
Nor e'er pretend to be;
We be three lads of fair Scotland,
Auld Maitland's sons, a' three!"

Thy first made all the table ring –
"By ----, Sir, but that is the thing!"

Yes, twenty years have come and fled
Since we two met, and time has shed
His riming honours o'er each brow –
My state the same, how changed art thou!
But every year yet overpast
I've loved thee dearer than the last.
For all the volumes thou hast wrote,
Those that are owned, and that are not,
Let these be conned even to a grain,
I've said it, and will say't again –
Who knows thee but by these alone,
The better half is still unknown.

I know thee well – no kinder breast
Beats for the woes of the distrest,
Bleeds for the wounds it cannot heal,
Or yearns more o'er thy country's weal.
Thy love embraces Britain o'er,
And spreads and radiates with her shore;
Scarce fading on her ocean's foam,
But still 'tis brightest nearer home,
Till those within its central rays,
Rejoicing, bask within the blaze.

Blessed be the act of sovereign grace,
That raised thee 'bove the rhyming race;
Blessed be the heart and head elate,
The noble generous estimate
That marked thy worth, and owned the hand
Resistless in its native land.
Bootless the waste of empty words,
Thy pen is worth ten thousand swords.

Long brook thy honours, gallant knight,
So firm of soul, so staunch of right;
For had thy form but reached its prime,
Free from mischance in early time,
No stouter sturdier arm of weir
Had wielded sword or battle spear.
For war thy boardly frame was born,
For battle shout, and bugle-horn;
Thy boyish feats, thy youthful dream —
How thy muse kindles at the theme!
Chance marred the path, or Heaven's decree;
How blessed for Scotland and for me!

Scarce sounds they name as't did before –
Walter the Abbot now no more:
Well, – let it be, – I'll not repine,
But love the title since 'tis thine.
Long brook thy honours, firm to stand
As Eildon rock; and that thy land,
The first e'er won by dint of rhyme,
May bear thy name till latest time,
And stretch from bourn of Abbot's-lea
To Philhope Cross, and Eildon Tree,
Is the heart's wish of one who's still
Thy grateful shepherd of the hill!

WHEN THE KYE COMES HAME

Come all ye jolly shepherds
That whistle through the glen,
I'll tell ye of a secret
That courtiers dinna ken:
What is the greatest bliss
That tongue o' man can name?
'Tis to woo a bonny lassie
When the kye comes hame,
When the kye comes hame,
When the kye comes hame,
'Tween the gloaming and the mirk,
When the kye comes hame.

'Tis not beneath the coronet
Nor canopy of state,
'Tis not on couch of velvet,
Nor arbour of the great –
'Tis beneath the spreading birk,
In the glen without a name,
Wi' a bonnie, bonnie lassie,
When the kye comes hame.
When the kye comes hame, etc.

There the blackbird bigs his nest
For the mate he lo'es to see,
And on the topmost bough,
Oh, a happy bird is he;
Where he pours his melting ditty,
And love is a' the theme,
And he'll woo his bonnie lassie
When the kye comes hame.
When the kye comes hame, etc.

When the blewart bears a pearl,
And the daisy turns a pea,
And the bonnie lucken gowan
Has fauldit up her e'e,
Then the laverock frae the blue lift
Drops down, an' thinks nae shame
To woo his bonnie lassie
When the kye comes hame.
When the kye comes hame, etc.

See yonder pawkie shepherd,
That lingers on the hill,
His ewes are in the fauld,
An' his lambs are lying still;
Yet he downa gang to bed,
For his heart is in a flame
To meet his bonnie lassie
When the kye comes hame.
When the kye comes hame, etc.

When the little wee bit heart
Rises high in the breast,
An' the little wee bit starn
Rises red, in the east,
Oh there's a joy sae dear,
That the heart can hardly frame,
Wi a bonnie, bonnie lassie,
When the kye comes hame!
When the kye comes hame, etc.

Then since all nature joins
In this love without alloy,
Oh, wha wad prove a traitor
To nature's dearest joy?
Oh wha wad chose a crown,
Wi' its perils and its fame,
And MISS his bonnie lassie
When the kye comes hame.
When the kye comes hame, etc.

CHARLIE IS MY DARLING

'Twas on a Monday morning,
Right early in the year,
That Charlie came to our town,
The young Chevalier.
An' Charlie is my darling,
My darling, my darling,
Charlie is my darling,
The young Chevalier.

As Charlie he came up the gate,
His face shone like the day;
I grat to see the lad come back
That had been lang away.
An' Charlie is my darling
My darling, my darling,
Charlie is my darling,
The young Chevalier.

Then ilka bonnie lassie sang,
As to the door she ran,
Our king shall hae his ain again,
An' Charlie is the man:
For Charlie he's my darling,
My darling, my darling,
Charlie is my darling,
The young Chevalier.

Outower yon moory mountain,
An' down the craigy glen,
Of naething else our lassies sing
But Charlie an' his men.
An' Charlie he's my darling,
My darling, my darling,
Charlie is my darling,
The young Chevalier.

Our Highland hearts are true an' leal,
An' glow without a stain;
Our Highland swords are metal keen,
An' Charlie he's our ain.
An Charlie he's my darling,
My darling, my darling,
Charlie is my darling,
The young Chevalier.

A BOY'S SONG

Where the pools are bright and deep,
Where the grey trout lies asleep,
Up the river and o'er the lea
That's the way for Billy and me.

Where the blackbird sings the latest,
Where the hawthorn blooms the sweetest,
Where the nestlings chirp and flee,
That's the way for Billy and me.

Where the mowers mow the cleanest,
Where the hay lies thick and greenest;
There to trace the homeward bee,
That's the way for Billy and me.

Where the hazel bank is steepest,
Where the shadow falls the deepest,
Where the clustering nuts fall free,
That's the way for Billy and me.

Why the boys should drive away
Little sweet maidens from the play,
Or love to banter and fight so well,
That's the thing I could never tell.

But this I know, I love to play,
Through the meadow, among the hay;
Up the water and o'er the lea,
That's the way for Billy and me.

MY LOVE SHE'S BUT A LASSIE YET

These verses were set to music, making
My Love She's But a Lassie Yet one of
Scotland's most popular songs.

My love she's but a lassie yet,
A lightsome, lovely lassie yet,
It scarce wad do to sit an' woo,
Down by the stream sae glassy yet,
But there's a braw time comin' yet
When we may gang a roamin' yet,
An' hint wi' glee o' joys to be,
When fa's the modest gloamin' yet.

She's neither proud not saucy yet,
She's neither plump nor gaucy yet,
But just a jinkin' bonnie blinkin';
Hilty, skilty lassie yet.
But O her artless smiles mair sweet
Than hinny or than marmalete;
An' right or wrang ere it be lang,
I'll bring her to a parly yet.

I'm jealous o' what blesses her,
The very breeze that kisses her;
The flow'ry beds on which she treads,
Though wae for ane that misses her.
Then O to meet my lassie yet,
Up in yon glen sae grassy yet;
For a' I see are nought to me,
Save her that's but a lassie yet.

Flora MacDonald's Farewell

Far over yon hills of the heather sae green,
  An' down by the correi that sings to the sea,
The bonnie young Flora sat sighing her lane,
  The dew on her plaid, and the tear in her e'e
She look'd at a boat wi' the breezes that swung
  Away, on the wave, like a bird of the main,
An' any as it lessen'd, she sighed an' she sung,
  Fareweel to the lad I shall ne'er see again!
Fareweel to my hero, the gallant an' young,
  Fareweel to the lad I shall ne'er see again.

The muircock that craws on the brows of Ben-Connal,
  He kens of his bed in a sweet mossy hame;
The eagle that soars o'er the cliffs of Clan-Ronald,
  Unawed and unhaunted, his eyry can claim;

The solan can sleep on the shelve of the shore,
  The cormorant roost on his rock of the sea,
But ah! there is one whose sad fate I deplore,
  Nor house, ha', nor hame, in this country has he –
The conflict is past, and our name is no more –
  There's nought left but sorrow for Scotland and me!

The target is torn from the arm of just,
   The helmet is cleft on the brow of the brave,
The claymore for ever in darkness must rust,
   But red is the sword of the stranger and slave;
The hoof of the horse, and the foot of the proud,
   Have trod o'er the plumes on the bonnet of blue:
Why slept the red bolt in the breast of the cloud
   When tyranny revell'd in blood of the true?
Fareweel, my young hero, the gallant and good;
   The crown of thy fathers is torn from thy brow!

THE STUARTS OF APPIN

I sing of a land that was famous of yore,
    The land of green Appin, the ward of the flood,
Where very grey cairn that broods o'er the shore,
    Marks grave of the royal, the valiant, or good:
The land where the strains of grey Ossain were framed –
    The land of fair Selma, the reign of Fingal –
And late of a race, that with tears must be named,
    The noble Clan Stuart, the bravest of all.
Oh-hon, an Righ! and the Stuarts of Appin!
    The gallant, devoted, old Stuarts of Appin!
        Their glory is o'er,
        For the clan is no more,
And the Sassenach sings on the hills of green Appin.

In spite of the Campbells, their might and renown,
    And all the proud files of Glenorchy and Lorn,
While one of the Stuarts held claim on the crown,
    His banner full boldly by Appin was borne.
And ne'er fell the Campbells in check or trepan,
    In all the Whig effords their power to renew,
But still on the Stuarts of Appin they ran,
    To wreak their proud wrath on the brave and the few.
Oh-hon, an righ! and the Stuarts of Appin, etc.

In the year of the Graham, while in oceans of blood
    The fields of the Campbells were gallantly flowing,
It was then that the Stuarts the foremost still stood,
    And paid back a share of the debt they were owing.
O proud Inverlochy! O day of renown!
    Since first the sun rose o'er the peaks of Cruachin,
Was ne'er such an host by such valour o'erthrown,
    Was ne'er such a day for the Stuarts of Appin!
Oh-hon, an righ! and the Stuarts of Appin, etc.

GEORGE MACDONALD

CHRISTMAS MEDITATION

He who by a mother's love
   Made the wandering world his own,
Every year comes from above,
   Comes the parted to atone,
   Binding Earth to the Father's throne.

Nay, thou comest every day!
   No, thou never didst depart!
Never hour hast been away!
   Always with us, Lord, thou art,
   Binding, binding heart to heart!

WILLIAM JULIUS MICKLE

THE SAILOR'S WIFE

And are ye sure the news is true?
  And are ye sure he's weel?
Is this a time to think o' wark?
  Ye jauds, fling bye your wheel!
Is this the time to spin a thread,
When Colin's at the door?
Rax down my cloak – I'll to the quay,
  And see him come ashore.
    For there's nae luck aboot the house,
      There's nae luck ava;
    Three's little pleasure in the house
      When our gudeman's awa'.

And gie to me my bigonet,
  My bishop's satin gown;
For I maun tell the bailie's wife
  That Colin's in the town.
My Turkey slippers maun gae on,
  My hose o' pearly blue, –
It's a' to pleasure our gudeman,
  For he's baith leal and true.

Rise up and mak' a clean fireside,
    Put on the muckle pot;
Gie little Kate her button gown,
    And Jock his Sunday coat;
And mak' their shoon as black as slaes,
    Their stockin's white as snaw, –
It's a' to please my ain gudeman –
    He likes to see them braw.

There's twa fat hens upon the bauk,
    Hae fed this month and mair;
Mak' haste and thraw their necks about,
    That Colin weel may fare;
And spread the table neat and clean –
    Gar ilka thing look braw;
For wha can tell how Colin fared
    When he was far awa'?

Sae true his heart, sae smooth his speech,
    His breath like caller air;
His very foot has music in't
    As he comes up the stair.
And will I see his face again?
    And will I hear him speak?
I'm downright dizzy wi' the thought, —
    In troth I'm like to greet!

If Colin's weel, and weel content,
    I hae nae mair to crave;
And gin I live to keep him sae,
    I'm blest aboon the lave.
And will I see his face again,
    And will I hear him speak? —
I'm downright dizzy wi' the thought, —
    In troth I'm like to greet!
        For there's nae luck aboot the house,
            There's nae luck ava;
        There's little pleasure in the house
            When our gudeman's awa'.

JAMES GRAHAM, MARQUIS OF MONTROSE

MY DEAR AND ONLY LOVE

My dear and only Love, I pray
  That little world of thee
Be govern'd by no other sway
  Than purest monarchy;
For if confusion have a part
  (Which virtuous souls abhor),
And hold a synod in thine heart,
  I'll never love thee more.

Like Alexander I will reign,
  And I will reign alone;
My thoughts did evermore disdain
  A rival on my throne.
He eigther fears his fate too much,
  Or his deserts are small,
That dares not put it to the touch,
  To gain or lose it all.

And in the empire of thine heart,
    Where I should solely be,
If others do pretend a part
    Or dare to vie with me,
Or if Committees *thou erect,*
    And go on such a score,
I'll laugh and sing at thy neglect,
    And never love thee more.

But if thou wilt prove faithful then,
    And constant of thy word,
I'll make thee glorious by my pen
    And famous by my sword;
I'll serve thee in such noble ways
    Was never heard before;
I'll crown and deck thee all with bays,
    And love thee more and more.

LADY NAIRNE
THE LAIRD O' COCKPEN

The Laird o' Cockpen, he's proud an' he's great,
His mind is ta'en up wi' things o' the State:
He wanted a wife, his braw house to keep;
But favour wi' wooin' ewas fashous to seek.

Down by the dyke-side a lady did dwell;
At his table-head he thought she'd look well –
McClish's ae daughter o' Claverse-ha' Lee,
A penniless lass wi' a lang pedigree.

His wig was weel pouther'd and as gude as new;
His waistcoat was white, his coat it was blue:
He put on a ring, a sword, and cock'd hat, –
And wha could refuse the Laird wi' a' that?

He took the grey mare, and rade cannily,
An' rapp'd at the yett o' Claverse-ha' Lee:
'Gae tell Mistress Jean to come speedily ben, –
She's wanted to speak to the Laird o' Cockpen.'

Mistress Jean was makin' the elder-flower wine:
'And what brings the Laird at sic a like time?'
She put aff her apron and on her silk goun,
Her mutch wi' red ribbons, and gaed awa doun.

An' when she cam' ben he bow'd fu' low;
An' what was his errand he soon let her know.
Amazed was the Laird when the lady said 'Na'; –
And wi' a laigh curtsey she turn'd awa.

Dumbfounder'd was he; nae sigh did he gie,
He mounted his mare, he rade cannily;
And aften he thought as he gaed thro' the glen,
'She's daft to refuse the Laird o' Cockpen!'

LADY ANNE LINDSAY

AULD ROBIN GRAY

When the sheep are in the fauld, and the kye at hame,
And a' the warld to rest are gane,
The waes o' my heart fa' in showers frae my e'e,
While my gudeman lies sound by me.

Young Jamie lo'ed me weel, and sought me for his bride;
But saving a croun he had naething else beside:
To make the croun a pund, young Jamie gaed to sea;
And the croun and the pund were baith for me.

He hadna been awa' a week but only twa,
When my father brak his arm, and the cow was stown awa';
My mother she fell sick, – and my Jamie at the sea –
And auld Robin Gray came a-courtin' me.

My father couldna work, and my mother couldna spin;
I toil'd day and night, but their bread I couldna win;
Auld Rob maintain'd them baith, and wi' tears in his e'e
Said, 'Jennie, for their sakes, O, marry me!'

My heart is said nay; I look'd for Jamie back;
But the wind it blew high, and the ship it was a wrack;
His ship it was a wrack – Why didna Jamie dee?
Or why do I live to cry, Wae's me!

My father urged me sair: my mother didna speak;
But she look'd in my face till my heart was like to break:
They gi'ed him my hand, tho' my heart was in the sea;
Sae auld Robin Gray he was gudeman to me.

I hadna been a wife a week but only four,
When mournfu' as I sat on the stane at the door,
I sae my Jamie's wraith, – for I couldna think it he,
Till he said, 'I'm come hame to marry thee.'

O sair, sair did we greet, and muckle did we say;
We took but ae kiss, and we tore ourselves away:
I wish that I were dead, but I'm no like to dee;
And why was I born to say, Wae's me!

I gang like a ghaist, and I carena to spin;
I daurna think on Jamie, for that wad be a sin;
But I'll do my best a gude wife aye to be,
For auld Robin Gray he is kind unto me.

JOHN LOGAN

TO THE CUCKOO

Hail, beauteous stranger of the grove!
  Thou messenger of Spring!
Now Heaven repairs thy rural seat,
  And woods thy welcome sing.

Wheat time the daisy decks the green,
  Thy certain voice we hear:
Hast thou a star to guide thy path,
  Or mark the rolling year?

Delightful visitant, with thee
  I hail the time of flowers;
And hear the sound of music sweet
  From birds among the bowers.

The schoolboy, wandering through the wood,
  To pull the primrose gay,
Starts the new voice of Spring to hear,
  And imitates thy lay.

What time the pea puts on the bloom,
  Thou fliest thy vocal vale —
An annual guest, in other lands,
  Another Spring to hail.

Sweet bird! thy bower is ever green,
  Thy sky is ever clear;
Thou hast no sorrow in thy song.
  No winter in thy year!

Alas! sweet bird! not so my fate;
  Dark scowling skys I see
Fast fathering round, and fraught with woe
  And ninety years to me.

O could I fly, I'd fly with thee!
  We'd make, with joyful wing,
Our annual visit o'er the globe —
  Companions of the Spring.

ROBERT FERGUSSON

THE DAFT DAYS

Now mirk December's dowie face
Glow'rs owre the rigs wi' sour grimace,
While, thro' his minimum o' space
      The bleer-e'ed sun,
Wi' blinkin' light and stealin' pace,
      His race doth run.

Frae naked groves nae birdie sings;
To shepherd's pipe nae hillock rings;
The breeze nae od'rous flavour brings
      Frae Borean cave;
And dwynin' Nature droops her wings,
      Wi' visage grave.

Mankind but scanty pleasure glean
Frae snawy hill or barren plain,
Whan Winter, 'midst his nippin' train,
      Wi' frozen spear,
Send drift owre a' his bleak domain,
      And guides the weir.

Auld Reikie! thou'rt the canty hole;
A bield for mony a cauldrife soul,
Wha snugly at thine ingle loll,
    Baith warm and couth;
While round they gar the bicker roll,
    To weet their mouth.

When merry Yule-day comes, I trow,
You'll scantlins find a hungry mou;
Sma' are our cares, our stamacks fou
    O gusty gear,
And kickshaws, strangers to our view
    Sin' fairn-year.

Ye browster wives! now busk ye braw,
And fling your sorrows far awa;
Then, come and gie's the tither blaw
    O' reaming ale,
Mair precious than the Well o' Spa,
    Our hearts to heal.

Then, tho' at odds wi' a' the warl,
Amang oursels we'll never quarrel;
Tho' Discord gie a canker'd snarl,
    To spoil our glee,
As lang's there's pith into the barrel,
        We'll drink and gree.

Fiddlers! your pins in temper fix,
And roset weel your fiddlesticks;
But banish vile Italian tricks
    Frae out your quorum;
Nor fortes wi' pianos mix; –
        Gie's Tullochgorum.

For nought can cheer the heart sae weel,
As can a canty Highland reel;
It even vivifies the heel
    To skip and dance:
Lifeless is he wha canna feel
        Its influence.

Let mirth abound; let social cheer
Invest the dawnin' o' the year;
Let blithesome Innocence appear,
  To crown our joy:
Nor Envy, wi' sarcastic sneer,
  Our bliss destroy.

And thou, great god of Aquavitæ!
Wha sways the empire o' this city; —
Whan fou, we're sometimes capernoity; —
  Be thou prepar'd
To hedge us frae that black banditti,
  The City Guard.

ALEXANDER SMITH

GLASGOW

Sing, Poet, 'tis a merry world;
That cottage smoke is rolled and curled
   In sport, that every moss
Is happy, every inch of soil;—
Before me runs a road of toil
   With my grave cut across.
Sing, trailing showers and breezy downs —
I know the tragic heart of towns.

City! I am true son of thine;
Ne'er dwelt I where great mornings shine
   Around the bleating pens;
Ne'er by the rivulets I strayed,
And ne'er upon my childhood weighed
   The silence of the glens.
Instead of shores where ocean beats,
I hear the ebb and flow of streets.

Black Labour draws his weary waves,
Into their secret-moaning caves;
   But with the morning light,

The sea again will overflow
With a long weary sound of woe,
    Again to faint in night.
Wave am I in that sea of woes;
Which, night and morning, ebbs and flows.

I dwelt within a gloomy court
Wherein did never sunbeam sport;
    Yet there my heart was stirr'd –
My very bood did dance and thrill,
When on my narrow window-sill,
    Spring lighted like a bird.
Poor flowers – I watched them pine for weeks,
With leaves as pale as human cheeks.

Afar, one summer, I was borne;
Through golden vapours of the morn,
    I heard the hills of sheep:
I trod with a wild ecstasy
The bright fringe of the living sea:
    And on a ruined keep
I sat, and watched an endless plain
Blacken beneath the gloom of rain.

O fair the lightly sprinkled waste,
O'er which a laughing shower has raced!
    O fair the April shoots!
O fair the woods on summer days,
While a blue hyacinthine haze
    Is dreaming round the roots!
In thee, O City! I discern
Another beauty, sad and stern.

Draw thy fierce streams of blinding ore,
Smite on a thousand anvils, roar
    Down to the harbour-bars;
Smoulder in smoky sunsets, flare
On rainy nights, with street and square
        Lie empty to the stars.
From terrace proud to alley base
I know thee as my mother's face.

When sunset bathes thee in his gold,
In wreaths of bronze thy sides are rolled,
    Thy smoke is dusky fire;
And, from the glory round thee poured,

A sunbeam like an angel's sword
   Shivers upon a spire.
Thus have I watched thee, Terror! Dream!
While the blue Night crept up the stream.

The wild Train plunges in the hills,
He shrieks across the midnight rills;
   Streams through the shifting glare,
The roar and flap of foundry fires,
That shake with light the sleeping shires;
   And on the moorlands bare,
He sees afar a crown of light
Hang o'er thee in the hollow night.

At midnight, when thy suburbs lie
As silent as a noonday sky,
   When larks with heat are mute,
I love to linger on thy bridge,
All lonely as a mountain ridge,
   Disturbed but by my foot;
While the black lazy stream beneath,
Steals from its far-off wilds of heath.

And through my heart, as through a dream,
Flows on that black disdainful stream;
    All scornfully it flows,
Between the huddled gloom of masts,
Silent as pines unvexed by blasts –
    'Tween lamps in streaming rows.
O wondrous sight! O stream of dread!
O long dark river of the dead!

Afar, the banner of the year
Unfurls: but dimply prisoned here,
    'Tis only when I greet
A dropt rose lying in my way,
A butterfly that flutters gay
    Athwart the noisy street,
I know the happy Summer smiles
Around thy suburbs, miles on miles.

All raptures of this mortal breath,
Solemnities of life and death,
    Dwell in thy noise alone:
Of me thou hast become a part –

Some kindred with my human heart.
   Lives in thy streets of stone;
For we have been familiar more
Than galley-slave and weary oar.

The beech is dipped in wine; the shower
Is burnished; on the swinging flower
   The latest bee doth sit.
The low sun stares through dust of gold,
And o'er the darkening heath and wold
   The large ghost-moth doth flit.
In every orchard Autumn stands,
With apples in his golden hands.

But all these sights and sounds are strange;
Then wherefore from thee should I range?
   Thou hast my kith and kin:
My childhood, youth, and manhood brave;
Thou hast an unforgotten grave
   Within thy central din.
A sacredness of love and death
Dwells in thy noise and smoky breath.

While o'er thy walls the darkness sails,
I lean against the churchyard rails;
*   Up in the midnight towers*
The belfried spire, the street is dead,
I hear in silence overhead
*   The clang of iron hours:*
It moves me not, I know her tomb
Is yonder in the shapeless gloom.

DOUGLAS OF FINGLAND

ANNIE LAURIE

Maxwellton braes are bonnie,
Where early fa's the dew,
And it's there that Annie Laurie
Gie'd me her promise true,
Gie'd me her promise true,
Which ne'er forgot will be;
And for bonnie Annie Laurie
I'd lay me doun and dee.

Her brow is like the snawdrift,
Her neck is like the swan;
Her face it is the fairest
That e'er the sun shone on;
That e'er the sun shone on,
And dark blue is her e'e;
And for bonnie Annie Laurie
I'd lay me doun and dee.

Like dew on the gowan lying,
Is the fa' o' her fairy feet;
And like winds in simmer sighing,
Her voice is low and sweet.
Her voice is low and sweet,
And she's a' the world to me;
And for bonnie Annie Laurie
I'd lay me down and dee.

ROBERT TANNAHILL
THE BRAES O' BALQUHIDDER

Will ye go, lassie go,
To the braes o' Balquhidder?
Where the blaeberries grow,
'Mang the bonnie bloomin' heather;
Where the deer and the rae,
Lightly bounding together,
Sport the lang summer day,
'Mang the braes o' Balquhidder?
Will ye go, lassie go,
To the braes o' Balquhidder?
Where the blaeberries grow,
'Mang the bonnie bloomin' heather.

I will twine thee a bow'r,
By the clear siller fountain,
An' I'll cover it o'er
Wi' the flowers o' the mountain;
I will range through the wilds,
An' the deep glens sae dreary.
An' return wi' their spoils
To the bower o' my deary.
Will ye go etc.

When the rude wintry win'
Idly raves round our dwellin',
An' the roar o' the linn
On the night breeze is swellin',
Sae merrily we'll sing,
As the storm rattles o'er us,
Till the dear sheeling ring
Wi' the light liltin' chorus.
Will ye go etc.

Now the simmer is in prime,
Wi' the flow'r's richly bloomin',
An' the wild mountain thyme
A' the moorlands perfumin',
To our dear native scenes
Let us journey together,
Where glad innocence reigns
'Mang the braes o' Blaquhidder.
Will ye go etc.

ANONYMOUS

SIR PATRICK SPENS

The King sits in Dunfermline town,
  Drinking the blude-red wine;
'O whare will I get a skeely skipper,
  To sail this new ship of mine?' –

O up and spake an eldern knight,
  Sat at the King's right knee, –
'Sir Patrick Spens is the best sailor,
  That ever sailed the sea.' –

Our King has written a braid letter,
  And seal'd it with his hand,
And sent it to Sir Patrick Spens,
  Was walking on the strand.

'To Noroway, to Noroway,
  To Noroway o'er the faem;
The King's daughter of Noroway,
  'Tis thou maun bring her hame.'

The first word that Sir Patrick read,
   Sae loud loud laughed he;
The neist word that Sir Patrick read,
   The tear blinded his ee.

'O wha is this has done this deed,
   And tauld the King o' me,
To send us out, at this time of the year,
   To sail upon the sea?

'Be it wind, be it weet, be it hail, be it sleet,
   Our ship must sail the faem;
The King's daughter of Noroway,
   'Tis we must fetch her hame.' –

They hoysed their sails on Monenday morn,
   Wi' a' the speed they may;
They hae landed in Noroway,
   Upon a Wodensday.

They hadna been a week, a week,
   In Noroway, but twae,
When that the lords o' Noroway,
   Began aloud to say, –

'Ye Scottishmen spend a' our King's gowd,
    And a' our Queenis fee.' –
'Ye lie, ye lie, ye liars loud!
    Fu' loud I hear ye lie;

'For I brought as much white monie,
    As gane my men and me,
And I brought a half-fou of gude red gowd,
    Out o'er the sea wi' me.

'Make ready, make ready, my merrymen a'!
    Our gude ship sails the morn.' –
'Now, ever alake, my master dear,
    I fear a deadly storm!

'I saw the new moon, late yestreen,
    Wi' the auld moon in her arm;
And, if we gang to sea, master,
    I fear we'll come to harm.'

They hadna sail'd a league, a league,
    A league but barely three,
When the lift grew dark, and the wind blew loud,
    And gurly grew the sea.

The ankers brak, and the topmasts lap,
　It was sic a deadly storm;
And the waves cam o'er the broken ship,
　Till a' her sides were torn.

'O where will I get a gude sailor,
　To take my helm in hand,
Till I get up to the tall top-mast,
　To see if I can spy land?' –

'O here am I, a sailor gude,
　To take the helm in hand,
Till you go up to the tall top-mast;
　But I fear you'll ne'er spy land.' –

He hadna gane a step, a step,
　A step but barely ane,
When a bout flew out of our goodly ship,
　And the salt sea it came in.

'Gae, fetch a web o' silken claith,
　Another o' the twine,
And wap them into our ship's side,
　And let nae the sea come in.' –

They fetch'd a web o' the silken claith,
    Another o' the twine,
And they wapp'd them round that gude ship's side,
    But still the sea cam in.

O laith, laith, were our gude Scots lords
    To weet their cork-heel'd shoon!
But lang or a' the play was play'd,
    They wat their hats aboon.

And mony was the feather bed,
    That flatter'd on the faem;
And mony was the gude lord's son,
    That never mair cam hame.

The ladyes wrang their fingers white,
    The maidens tore their hair,
A' for the sake of their true loves;
    For them they'll see nae mair.

O lang, lang, may the ladyes sit,
    Wi' their fans into their hand,
Before they see Sir Patrick Spens
    Come sailing to the strand!

And lang, lang, may the maidens sit,
    With their gowd kaims in their hair,
A' waiting for their ain dear loves!
    For them they'll see nae mair.

Half-owre, half-owre to Aberdour,
    'Tis fifty fathoms deep,
And there lies gude Sir Patrick Spens,
    Wi' the Scots lords at his feet.

THE BONNY EARL O' MORAY

Ye Highlands and ye Lawlands,
  O where hae ye been?
They hae slain the Earl o' Moray,
  And hae laid him on the green.

Now wae be to thee, Huntley!
  And whairfore did ye sae!
I bade you bring him wi' you,
  But forbade you him to slay.

He was a braw gallant,
  And he rid at the ring;
And the bonny Earl o' Moray,
  O he might hae been a king!

He was a braw gallant,
    And he play'd at the ba';
And the bonny Earl o' Moray
    Was the flower amang them a'!

He was a braw gallant,
    And he play'd at the gluve;
And the bonny Earl o' Moray,
    O he was the Queen's luve!

O lang will his Lady
    Look owre the Castle Downe,
Ere she see the Earl o' Moray
    Come sounding through the town!

HELEN OF KIRKCONNELL

I wish I were where Helen lies,
Night and day on me she cries;
O that I were where Helen lies,
*   On fair Kirkconnell lea!*

Curst be the heart that thought the thought,
And curst the hand that fired the shot,
When in my arms burd Helen dropt,
*   And died to succour me!*

O think na ye my heart was sair,
When my Love dropp'd and spak nae mair!
There did she swoon wi' meikle care,
*   On fair Kirkconnell lea.*

As I went down the water side,
None but my foe to be my guide,
None but my foe to be my guide,
*   On fair Kirkconnell lea;*

I lighted down my sword to draw,
I hackèd him in pieces sma',
I hackèd him in pieces sma',
  For her sake that died for me.

O Helen fair, beyond compare!
I'll mak a garland o' thy hair,
Shall bind my heart for evermair,
  Until the day I dee!

O that I were where Helen lies!
Night and day on me she cries;
Out of my bed she bids me rise,
  Says, 'Haste, and come to me!'

O Helen fair! O Helen chaste!
If I were with thee, I'd be blest,
Where thou lies low an' taks thy rest,
  On fair Kirkconnell lea.

I wish my grave were growing green,
A winding-sheet drawn owre my een,
And I in Helen's arms lying,
*   On fair Kirkconnell lea.*

I wish I were where Helen lies!
Night and day on me she cries;
And I am weary of the skies,
*   For her sake that died for me.*

THE WIFE OF USHER'S WELL

There lived a wife at Usher's well,
    And a wealthy wife was she;
She had three stout and stalwart sons,
    And sent them o'er the sea.

They hadna been a week from her,
    A week but barely ane,
When word came to the carline wife
    That her three sons were gane.

They hadna been a week from her,
    A week but barely three,
When word came to the carline wife
    That her sons she'd never see.

'I wish the wind may never cease,
    Nor fashes in the flood,
Till my three sons come hame to me
    In earthly flesh and blood!'

It fell about the Martinmas,
  When nights are lang and mirk,
The carline wife's three sons came hame,
  And their hats were o' the birk.

It neither grew in syke nor ditch,
  Nor yet in ony sheugh;
But at the gates o' Paradise
  That birk grew fair eneugh.

'Blow up the fire, my maidens!
  Bring water from the well!
For a' my house shall feast this night,
  Since my three sons are well.'

And she has made to them a bed,
  She's made it large and wide;
And she's ta'en her mantle her about,
  Sat down at the bedside.

Up then crew the red, red cock,
  And up and crew the gray;
The eldest to the youngest said,
  ''Tis time we were away.'

The cock he hadna craw'd but once,
   And clapp'd his wings at a',
When the youngest to the eldest said,
   'Brother, we must awa'.

'The cock doth craw, the day doth daw,
   The channerin' worm doth chide;
Gin we be miss'd out o' our place,
   A sair pain we maun bide.' –

'Lie still, lie still but a little wee while,
   Lie still but if we may;
Gin my mother should miss us when she wakes,
   She'll go mad ere it be day.' –

'Fare ye weel, my mother dear!
   Fareweel to barn and byre!
And fare ye weel, the bonny lass
   That kindles my mother's fire!'

THE TWA BROTHERS

There were twa brethren in the north,
*   They went to school thegithar;*
The one unto the other said,
*   Will you try a warsle afore?*

They wrestled up, they wrestled down,
*   Till Sir John fell to the ground,*
And there was a knife in Sir Willie's pouch,
*   Gied him a deadlie wound.*

'Oh brither dear, take me on your back,
*   Carry me to yon burn clear,*
And wash the blood from off my wound,
*   And it will bleed nae mair.'*

He took him up upon his back,
*   Carried him to yon burn clear,*
And washd the blood from off his wound,
*   And aye it bled the mair.*

'Oh brother dear, take me on your back,
    Carry me to yon kirk-yard,
And dig a grave baith wide and deep,
    And lay my body there.'

He's taen him up upon his back,
    Carried him to yon kirk-yard,
And dug a grave both deep and wide,
    And laid his body there.

'But what will I say to my father dear,
    Should he chance to say, Willie, whar's John?'
'Oh say that he's to England gone,
    To buy him a cask of wine.'

'And what shall I say to my mother dear,
    Should she chance to say, Willie, whar's John?'
'Oh say that he's to England gone,
    To buy her a new silk gown.'

'And what will I say to my sister dear,
    Should she chance to say, Willie, whar's John?'
'Oh say that he's to England gone,
    To buy her a wedding ring.'

'*What will I say to her you loe dear,*
  Should she cry, Why tarries my John?'
'*Oh tell her I lie in fair Kirk-land,*
  And home will never come'